The Five Be's

Second Edition

Mickey Addison

Lead the Way Media

Kailua, Hawaii

The Five Be's Second Edition

Cover image licensed through Canva.com

ISBN: 978-0-9960193-2-3 (First Edition, The 5 Be's for Starting Out)

ISBN: 978-0-9960193-6-1 Second Edition

Published by: Lead the Way Media, Kailua, Hawaii

mickey@leadthewaymedia.com

This book is available through Lulu.com, Amazon, and via Mickey's website at mickeyaddison.com in paperback and e-book formats. Order forms are also in the back of the book.

For the Air Force Noncommissioned Officers Corps: today's heroes who daily turn young people into leaders and tomorrow's heroes.

Figures

Figure 1. Voyager spacecraft Trajectories.... 29

Figure 2. The Golden Mean 37

Figure 3. Maslow's hierarchy of needs 57

Figure 4. A model of the human person 64

Figure 5. Map of Wake Island..................... 96

Figure 6. Gen George S. Patton, Jr., USA 97

Contents

Thank You x

The Second Edition xi

About this Book xiii

Introduction 1

Be Proud 7

    Everyone Can Be Proud of Something 11

    Esprit de Corps 13

    Looking Inside for the Good 16

    Authentic Pride 19

Be Free 23

Be Virtuous 33

    Prudence 39

    Justice 43

    Temperance 45

    Fortitude 50

    Wrapping Up Virtue 53

Be Balanced 55

    The Human in Three Parts 60

    The Body 66

The Mind.................................... 70

The Spirit.................................... 74

Be Courageous............................... 79

Physical Courage 82

Moral Courage............................. 89

Summing It Up 101

Index...109

End Notes 111

Thank You

Thanks to all those who contributed, knowingly or unknowingly, to this book. To the many mentors who encouraged me to be the best man I could be, thank you for your support. For all my bosses and teammates who endured my rants, my wild ideas, and my unbridled enthusiasm, thank you for your patience!

A special thanks to the noncommissioned officers who taught me so much about leadership and how to be an officer—many of you will never know the impact you had on me, but it was and is significant.

Finally, thank you to my wife who has stood by me and encouraged me through my entire adult life. You are the reason I have the courage to face the day.

Forward to the Second Edition

This book began as a set of sticky notes.

Truly! From those humble beginnings, *The Five Be's* has become by far my most popular talk as a professional speaker. I originally wrote this book and the talk it sprang from for young adults just starting out in life. However, I've been encouraged by the enthusiastic reception from audiences of all ages. Since first published in 2015, *The 5 Be's for Starting Out*, I've presented these ideas to audiences ranging from middle schoolers to C-suite executives. It's been fabulous to see how much people identify with the ideals behind *The Five Be's* at every age and state of life. I believe there's a reason for this universal appeal.

The appeal of *The Five Be's* can be summed up in one word: **authenticity**. In our modern age where we experience so much the world through computer screens, people want something that's real. I believe that's the reason for the current explosion of "craft" and "hand-made" items ranging from furniture to spirits. Our human spirit hungers for connection, for purpose, and for truth.

The Five Be's is my answer to that search: a positive vision of what an authentic and connected person looks like, and the values that guide their life. *The Five Be's* is a prescription for a healthy and successful life: to be fully human. That connection to the world and the people around us is the reason we selected a farmhouse for the cover.

The farmhouse and the open field speaks to connection with the earth and the seasons. An untilled field is ready to be worked and the promise of the harvest that follows. It's not shiny and new, which speaks to the trials of life and the passage of time. The simplicity of the image reminds us we really need very little to be happy. It's authentic, it's connected, it's real.

Authenticity is the core what *The Five Be's* is really all about. Becoming and remaining a "fully formed" human being in the face of a torrent of things that would keep us from that being. It's a straightforward guide to life.

About this Book

This book is about how to live a full, successful, and happy life.

This is not a leadership book, yet good leaders practice these principles and espouse many of these ideas. It's not a religious book, although you're sure to see some common religious themes in some of the ideas presented. It's not a moralist's view, although you can certainly use the principles I describe to make good moral choices.

This book is a positive vision of who I would like to be, and who I want the ones around me to be. Do I always "walk the talk"? Of course, I don't; few do. But I can say that each time I haven't lived up to my own ideals, I've regretted it. The Five Be's is a vision of a person who can face the world and live in it without being swept away by it. It's who I want to be.

Introduction

---

*Whatever you are, be a good
one.*

\- Abraham Lincoln

I stood in front of a group of sleepy young Airmen at the First Term Airmen Center (FTAC) as they waited to hear what the old colonel had to say. With few exceptions, they were all approximately 19 years old and living away from home for the first time in their lives. They had all volunteered to serve their country in a time of war. Most of them were in kindergarten or elementary school during the 9/11 attacks. Their reasons for joining the military were as varied as their backgrounds: patriotism, opportunity, adventure, and family tradition. The same as soldiers from any age.

Before they appeared in their new Air Force blue uniforms in that FTAC classroom, they had successfully completed 12 weeks of Air Force Basic Military Training. In addition, they had attended Air Force Technical Training to learn the skills each would employ in their Air Force Specialty.

For their first six months in the Air Force, they'd heard their leaders give them a lot of "don'ts." It wasn't just the Air Force Military Training Instructors who had told them "don't"; they have been hearing that word throughout their lives: from parents, from teachers, from coaches, and even from peers.

As we raise young people into adulthood, we put a great deal of effort into setting boundaries. In fact, most of what young people hear as they grow is a list of "don'ts." When we're very young, we hear "Don't throw food on the floor," "Don't speak disrespectfully to your elders," and "Don't take toys away from your friends." As we grow, the "don'ts" begin to pile up: don't play in the street, don't forget your manners, and don't use bad language. Even in adulthood,

> *We are what we repeatedly do; excellence, then, is not an act but a habit.*
>
> - Aristotle

we are inundated with "don'ts" regarding our behavior: don't say those words, don't wear those clothes, don't eat this, and don't touch that.

All these "don'ts" form the boundaries of acceptable behavior. When reasonably imposed, boundaries are a necessary part of establishing what's appropriate and acceptable. Manners, after all, are intended to make everyone comfortable, so that each person's dignity and feelings are safeguarded. All human groupings develop norms for behavior that each group member is expected to adhere to. They vary in complexity and formality, but norms, boundaries, or "don'ts" are common. Of course, we can overdo boundary setting. When there are too many boundaries, then it becomes tyranny. In general, however, boundaries and standards of behavior ("manners") are necessary to the function of any human society.

What's generally left unsaid when establishing our group norms is a target to focus on. It's not sufficient to merely describe the outside boundaries of the target; you also must show people what the bull's-eye looks like. That's what this book is all about.

People can function in a world of "do's" and "don'ts," but knowing what to do and what not to do only describes external behavior. What people, particularly young people, really need is a vision of who they should want to be. With that vision, people are then empowered to reach for something rather than merely avoiding something.

To illustrate that point, imagine the following situation:

You're in a pitch-black room with the task of finding a door somewhere in the room. What would you do? Most people would find the walls first, feeling their way slowly around the walls until they found the door, then opening the door to exit. But what if the exit was really a trap door set in the floor? Or a staircase in the center of the room? What if the walls gave way with the slightest pressure leaving you groping in the dark? Simply being told there is a door in the room isn't enough information to find the door. There's even less of a chance if the walls are unstable.

Giving a person a vision of who we want them to be is like turning on an exit light in that imaginary room. The light will dimly illuminate the way, and give them a direction to walk toward. It could even be bright enough to illuminate the entire room.

What this thought experiment illustrates, is the need for both boundaries and a target: standards of behavior and a positive vision of who we should want to be.

That's what I wanted to give those bright young Airmen at FTAC: a positive vision of who I want them to be. A vision of a person who is healthy, integrated, balanced and free—the kind of person who can be proud of who they are, as we are proud of them. I wanted to give them a vision to aim for, so they could grow into the kind of people others would want to follow.

And now I offer to you that same vision of who I wanted them to be, and the kind of person I want to be as well.

Be Proud

Vanity and pride are different things, though the words are often used synonymously. A person may be proud without being vain. Pride relates more to our opinion of ourselves; vanity, to what we would have others think of us.

\- Jane Austen

Airmen take a lot of ribbing from our fellow warriors for the supposedly "soft" life they live compared to the other Services. It's not true, of course. Just like all modern warriors, Airmen work in a variety of environments ranging from pressurized cockpits at the threshold of space, to austere battlefields in far flung places, and of course, air conditioned offices as well. But the myth of the "easy" Air Force persists in some circles.

It's the same sort of stereotyping that happens within all the armed services. Many a joke told in joint military commands begins with the opening line, "A Soldier, a Sailor, a Marine, and an Airman walk into a bar..." While it's fun to tease each other, trust me when I say that most Airmen don't spend their days playing golf, lounging by the pool, or punching keyboards in air-conditioned offices. We are warriors, and we are proud of our Service, and proud to be part of the Joint Team.

When I faced those young Airmen new to the Air Force, I wanted them to understand the organization they joined was not the caricature they might have heard about from family members or classmates at joint technical schools. Everyone should be proud of their Service, so I began the discussion about who I wanted them to be by telling them about the Air

Force they'd joined. My speech went something like this:

You have joined the United States Air Force: the mightiest military force in the history of the planet. We can go anywhere on the planet we choose to go, and either look at it, feed it, or kill it. One Air Force bomber wing can devastate an entire country, and a single Air Force F-35 can put a 2,000-pound weapon into a specific window of a specific building to destroy a specific target on order from the President. When Navy SEALS or Army Rangers get into trouble, they call Air Force gunships and pararescuemen to come to their aid. We fly in space; we command two-thirds of America's nuclear arsenal. Control of the ground and sea is contingent upon control of the air. The United States Air Force controls the air.

We are part of a joint team, and each Service brings their own special skills and competencies to bear to defend America and her allies. We don't brag and we don't denigrate our joint teammates. Good-natured ribbing is fine and even healthy, but never let friendly competition turn into running someone else down. Be proud to be an Airman, be proud of your teammates, and be proud of your contribution to the joint team.

It was a little bit of cheerleading for our own Service, of course, but the goal was to instill a sense of pride into these new Airmen. Being aware of the way we poke fun at each other in the military, my aim was to insulate those young people from becoming a self-fulfilling stereotype. I want and expect Airmen to be proud of the Air Force, as I want and expect Marines, Soldiers, and Sailors to be proud of their branches of the Service. I never want that pride to turn into contempt for our teammates.

Being proud of who you are should not be confined to the wearing of a uniform. I believe everyone should take pride in who they are and what they're capable of becoming. While the genesis of "Be Proud" started with "Be Proud of Being an Airman," the principle extends to a broader perspective, "Be Proud of Who You Are."

Everyone Can Be Proud of Something

The saddest people I've ever met were those who doubted their own self-worth. Sometimes, because of their own poor choices, but, more often, because another person had beaten them down, the person without self-esteem looks in the mirror and sees nothing of value.

Experts on human behavior write volumes on how to increase our self-esteem or pride in ourselves. Everyone has a theory about how to improve it. While there are plenty of gimmicks out there, the only true sense of self-worth is the one that grows from within, based on the real and potential gifts in a person. To put it another way, a person can repeat, "I'm good enough, I'm smart enough" to himself all day while continuing to be a doormat. No one can rely on external influences and gimmicks; each of us must seize on something within ourselves. Even an esprit de corps expertly generated by a charismatic leader can only go so far. At some point, each individual should internalize their**Error! Bookmark not defined.** pride in their team and make it their own.

The purpose of The Five Be's is to help you be free and healthy so you can be the person you want to be.

Everyone has something they can be proud of, and their mentors and friends should encourage them to find those things within them. For some, it's their achievements and their knowledge and know-how. For others, their sense of pride and self-worth comes from their relationships or how they serve others. A person can be proud of their family, or their company's accomplishments; they can be proud of the mission of their company. The point is each person has *something* for which they can be proud. The task of mentors, parents, and leaders is to help individuals find their own strength by helping them find something that gives a sense of internal pride and self-worth.

Esprit de Corps

Before we begin the discussion on helping people find their own strengths, it's important to address the external aspects of "pride." In the military, as illustrated in my Airman" speech to the FTAC Airmen, it's virtuous for individuals to subordinate their own needs to that of the group. The Air Force Core Value of *"Service Before Self" embodies this idea.* For mentors, coaches, and leaders in every type of organization, esprit de corps builds team cohesion and imparts a sense of belonging to the group. *Esprit de corps,* literally "spirit of the body," is the collective pride in the larger group. It is a necessary and desirable starting point used to assemble a group of people into a team to accomplish a shared goal.

Helping our new Airmen find some pride in their organization was the reason I began my speech to the FTAC Airmen the way I did. Reminding them about the might of the Service they volunteered to join. For the young Airmen to take their service seriously, they needed to take their Air Force seriously. *Esprit de corps* helps a person take pride in their group membership, enabling them to overcome the natural and human tendency of placing individual interests before that of the group.

Furthermore, the subordination of an individual's needs will assist that group member's personal growth. The principle is the same in many walks of life, such as athletics, religion, business, or art. Any time we learn to delay gratification for the good of others, we gain the opportunity to learn something new about ourselves and, as a side effect, advance the shared goals of the group.

This is pride experienced from group participation in the best case. Like all things, divergence to either extreme can create vice. In the extreme, if individuals twist pride into fanaticism. If pride in one's group results in the subordination of all good outside of the group, then people become fanatics.

Fanatics are capable of great harm, either through violence or just plain ugliness. It's the same vice that generates bullying in high school and, at its most extreme, war crimes like ethnic cleansing. On the other end of the scale, the wrong sort of pride in the group creates a user of people, where they spend their lives in subordination to the group to the exclusion of all other good. This is the kind of pride that results in a stereotypical "salaryman" [1] who neglects his family for work.

Therefore, mentors and leaders should appreciate the power of external motivation and *esprit de corps*, and use that power only for good—the good of the team *and* the good of the individual.

Esprit de corps should inspire us to achieve, to become virtuous, and to become better people.

Looking Inside for the Good

Externals influences are powerful, but they only go so far. At some point, people must find meaning within themselves. Healthy people accomplish more personally and professionally. If we strive to raise healthy people, we must first help them find their own self-worth.

Each person, regardless of status, wealth, beauty, or even accomplishment has value because he or she is a unique human being with inherent self-worth. While an individual can distinguish him or herself by unique characteristics, people must never lose sight of the fact that they all have something to contribute. Sometimes, they confuse "self-worth" with "self-esteem."

It's useful to do some word analysis to clearly differentiate between the two concepts of worth and esteem.

The Oxford Dictionary defines worth and esteem as, respectively:

Worth: Sufficiently good, important, or interesting to justify a specified action; deserving to be treated or regarded in the way specified.

Esteem: Respect and admiration, typically for a person.

The difference between the two words is subtle, but important. Your self-worth is inherent, while esteem depends on an opinion given by someone else. For example, an athlete can have very high self-worth, being a kind or generous person, but be held very low esteem for reasons outside their control. Your "self-worth" is different. It's *independent* of what others think of you or even what you think of yourself – human beings have inherent worth because we are "fearfully and wonderfully made." The idea of human dignity and worth is universal, and held by all major faiths and moral systems.

Naturally, we understand the idea of the innate worth of a human being in general, but a great number of people have difficulty understanding that *they* are valuable. We don't accept bullying, we demand equal pay for equal work, we rebel at unfair play in sports, and we are quick to defend the innocent or weak from harm. But somehow, we have a difficult time transferring that innate sense of another's worth, into accepting our own self-worth.

I recently saw a great television commercial produced by a popular soap manufacturer that perfectly illustrates the point of recognizing our own blind spots. In the commercial, the manufacturer asked several women to describe themselves to a forensic sketch artist. In their descriptions, the women proceeded to point out all their flaws as part of the descriptive process.

After the women left the room, a second group entered the room, and proceeded to describe the first group of subjects. The members of the second group had just met the subjects, and had spent some time getting to know them. They pointed out the good things, such as "a nice smile" or "bright eyes." The subjects then returned to view the two drawings the artist had created.

The sketches the artists created using the women's self-descriptions were harsh and stark with little beauty. However, the portraits generated by the descriptions from others showed the women as they're seen by rest of the world – interesting and charismatic, even beautiful.

Self-worth, therefore, isn't merely respecting yourself or accepting adulation from others. It's realizing that you have worth, because you're inherently equal in dignity to every other person. We're not all equal in rank, social status, looks, or ability, but we're all equal in dignity. Recognizing that you have something to offer, no matter what it might be, is recognition of your own inherent value.

Authentic Pride

Authentic pride should never tear someone down; rather, authentic pride is about carrying oneself with dignity while recognizing the same dignity in others.

Returning to the example I used with the Airmen, I reminded them that friendly ribbing between the military Services is good for morale and teamwork, but when that friendly ribbing turns mean-spirited, it becomes a problem. I call that "counterfeit pride." While being insistent on not allowing others to tear us down (or our teammates), we must refuse to follow suit. Our goal should never be to build ourselves up by tearing them down.

There is some science supporting the idea of "authentic pride" vs. "counterfeit pride." In a 2007 study, University of British Columbia, Assistant Professor Jessica Tracy[2] and University of California Davis, Professor Richard Robins, found that authentic pride in oneself is a key component to well-being. In a two-year study conducted from 2003 to 2005 in rural Toussiana, Burkina Faso, Tracy showed photos of Americans and West Africans to Burkinabe subjects who could neither read nor write. The test subjects then labeled each photo with a perceived emotion: anger, disgust, fear, happiness, sadness, or surprise. Tracy discovered that there was a basic human ability, regardless of culture or education, to identify pride within the photos.

Furthermore, Tracy could distinguish two different types of pride: "Authentic" and "Hubristic." Authentic pride is the preferred type, pride in accomplishment, the shared pride of a championship sports team or making the honor roll. Authentic pride helps to reinforce self-worth and promote confidence, and a yearning to strive for greater achievement.

"Hubristic pride" or "counterfeit pride," as I call it, is just the opposite. It drags others down, causing interpersonal conflict. Counterfeit pride contributes to an inflated ego, and prevents an individual from having authentic self-worth.

> *Be like the Alamihi Crab,*
> *not the A'ama Crab!*
>
> - Hawaiian Proverb

In Hawaii, there two types of crabs that could be used as the "poster crabs" for pride. A bucket full of A'ama Crabs will fight over each other to climb out, pushing and shoving each other to gain an escape advantage. As soon as one crab starts to get out of the bucket, another will pull him back in. None of the crabs can escape the bucket.

The Alamihi Crab is different. They will build a ladder with their own bodies, and *pull each other out*. That's what authentic pride - real self-worth - does for us. It not only builds our own confidence, it builds up others too. Be an Alamihi Crab!

Be Free

---

*Freedom consists not in
doing what we like, but in
having the right to do what we
ought.*

\- John Paul II

Freedom is a word often misused in our current vocabulary. We view our "freedoms" in such a broad manner that the word sometimes loses its meaning. Particularly in the case of young people, "freedom" is sometimes construed as synonymous with "doing whatever I like." That's not authentic freedom. Authentic freedom is being able to choose what's good for you, yet remaining unencumbered by things that prevent you from being healthy. In fact, unbounded freedom to do whatever I want whenever I want is not freedom; it is license.

It's not a radical concept, the idea that freedom is bound by responsibilities and limits; in fact, it's preserved in our system of laws and our notion of justice. We regulate speech and assembly both for the common good and for the individual's good. People are not permitted to gather to foment violence, and we don't allow a person to run into a theater and shout "fire" unless there's really a fire. Ideally, our laws are constructed to both protect the common good, and safeguard individual liberty. However, even the freedom we enjoy as Americans is not unfettered liberty. We are free, but we do not have license to do anything we want.

Authentic freedom is an individual's ability to choose what is good without being impeded or bound, be it an internal or external restriction. If an individual's appetites or another person's demands prevent the individual from making good choices, then we can objectively say that the individual is not free.

> *For to be free is not merely to cast off one's chains, but to live in a way that respects and enhances the freedom of others.*
>
> - Nelson Mandela

For example, if a person is addicted to a behavior or substance, then the addiction is ruling the person's life, not freedom of choice. The extreme example of course is drug abuse, but there are many more things that can control someone's life, preventing them from choosing what's best for them. Overeating will keep a person from exercising properly and maintaining physical health; working excessive hours will limit interaction with family and friends; viewing pornography debases a person's view on sex and damages relationships. The list goes on. When it comes to vices and addictions, there are literally "a million of them" out there. To sum it up, if your appetites control you, then you are not free.

They're not called "vices" for nothing, and there's certainly nothing glamorous about them.

Addiction is a massive worldwide problem, with millions bound to some "force" other than the ability to choose what's best for them. According to a 2014 report by the U.S. Department of Health and Human Services[3], addiction to tobacco, alcohol, and illicit drugs cost $700 million in health care. In 2012, 4.3 million Americans met the clinical criteria for dependence or abuse of marijuana in the previous year.[4]

> *What fascinates me about addiction and obsessive behavior is that people would choose an altered state of consciousness that's toxic and ostensibly destroys most aspects of your normal life, because for a brief moment you feel okay.*
>
> - Moby, musician-songwriter

Drug and alcohol dependence are easy targets and well known, but what about other addictions? In a 2008 University of Pittsburgh study, 9% of the 3,034 participants showed signs of video game addiction[5,6] Debt can be similarly crushing to our freedom. In 2015, the Federal Reserve reported Americans owed a whopping $3.34 trillion in consumer debt. If people are depending on high interest loans or being forced to make certain choices because of their debt, can we truly say they are free?

Expenses born by "society" at large such as increased health care costs to treat addicts, are not the only costs to surrendering your freedom. Addiction has personal costs as well. People who suffer from addictions report that their addictions control their day-to-day activities and actions, restricting the ability to think or act on any impulse except obtaining the next fix. Many of these unfortunate people end up abandoning their family, careers, friends, and even their homes due to the overriding addiction. I don't think anyone would disagree that someone who's addicted is not free.

This is such a problem that we have an entire industry dedicated to helping people overcome addictions. There are thousands of addiction rehabilitation programs throughout the country – from the usual addictions like drugs and alcohol to Internet and video game addiction. The common theme is that something becomes a problem when it takes command of a person's life.

Note I use the terms demands or appetites here with the implication they are unreasonable or unhealthy. That's not to be confused with having rules or even laws that govern behavior. Rules do not make a person fettered; in fact, we need rules to help maintain our freedom. I know that sounds backwards, but let me give you two examples.

First, consider the case of gravity. Naturally, gravity seems to be something that only holds us bound to the Earth and restricts our movement. However, gravity is the real reason we have physical freedom of movement. We begin with some basic physics – all objects with mass have gravity. Therefore, the Sun, Earth, even your own body have some measure of gravity. According to Newton's Laws of Motion, an object at rest or in motion won't change its direction or speed unless something acts on it. Imagine an astronaut falls through a black hole and into a parallel universe with no gravity (laws). Without the "Law" of gravity, our poor astronaut would be stuck traveling in whatever direction he happened to be traveling when he appeared, or stuck wherever he happened to be, until he collides with something. However, in a universe with a "Law" of gravity, we have the freedom to move where we like and can even travel through outer space by using gravity to accelerate spacecraft around planets. Without gravity, there's no freedom. What was originally perceived as a constraint of freedom has been an enabler of freedom to travel to the stars from the beginning.

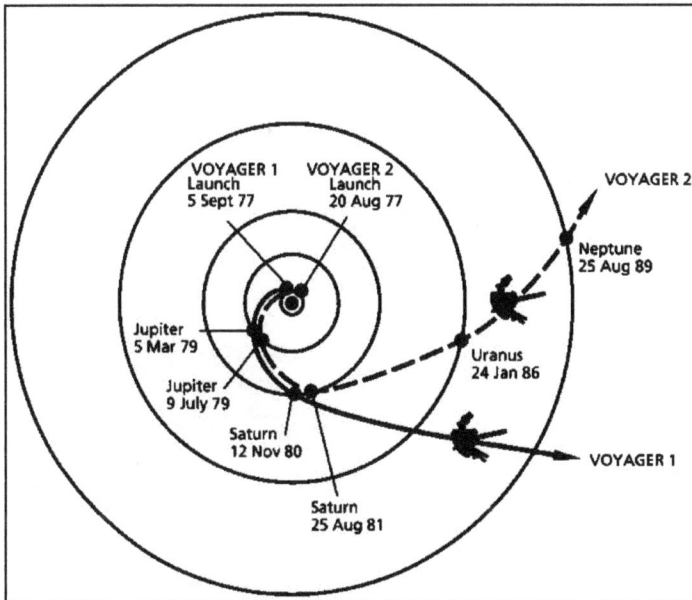

Figure 1. A diagram of the trajectories that enabled NASA's twin Voyager spacecraft to escape the solar system. (NASA, 1977)

For the second example, we will look at traffic controls, which are tools such as traffic signals, signage, speed limits, and pavement markings. Traffic controls restrict the flow of vehicular traffic on roads and highways to comply with specific safety rules and guidelines. A superficial look at traffic controls would imply that traffic controls restrict a driver's freedom, but the opposite is the case. Imagine how dangerous roads would be without speed limits, signage, or lane markings.

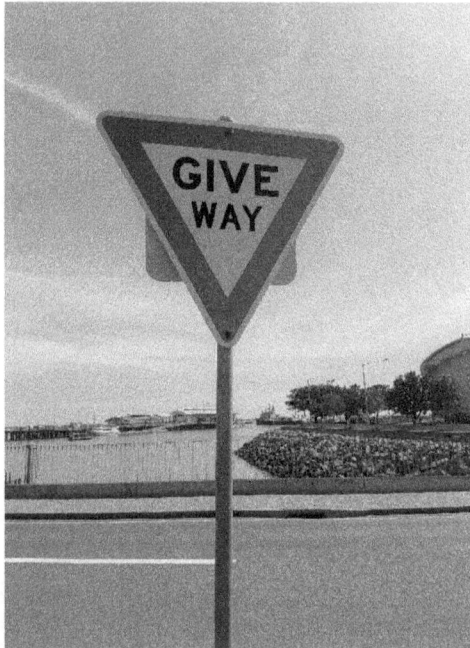

However, with appropriate traffic controls, we have the freedom to safely travel wherever we like. We can feel safe traveling at high speeds on the highway since we know that our fellow motorists will also be following the guidelines ensuring safe travel for all. Appropriate behavioral controls permit us to remain free and, in this case, unharmed.

The opposite of freedom is not "just" confinement or restriction. As we will discuss in the next section, Aristotle's philosophy of the Golden Mean, virtue lies in the middle between the extremes of vice.

Therefore, on one end of the "freedom continuum" lies slavery, and on the other lies license. Just as slavery is the abuse of freedom to hold another unjustly bound, license, likewise, is an abuse of freedom since it binds our own will to our appetites or passions. The newspaper is brimming with stories of people who abused their own freedom either through self-abuse or by allowing others to abuse them. "Excessive freedom" is as much a problem as a complete lack of freedom, and in fact ends up in the same place: slavery. On the ends of the "freedom continuum" is slavery to others and slavery to appetites – both are self-destructive.

As a military officer, I often remind my Airmen that the Air Force doesn't set standards of behavior (i.e., regulations) to hinder their freedom. Rather, we set standards of behavior to keep them safe and healthy, ready to accomplish our mission – to have the defense of our countrymen in our hands is a serious responsibility.

When Airmen violate these standards, leaders must do their duty and hold them accountable – this is justice. Furthermore, being held accountable is actually good for morale. The consequences for violating military standards range from minor to severe, depending on the seriousness of the offense, and they always entail some sort of penalty such as a fine, extra duty, or demotion of rank. When others see an offender receive their just deserts for violating the rules or the law, it reinforces their confidence in their leaders and each other.

To summarize, true freedom does not come at someone else's expense, and true freedom doesn't result from selfishness or self-centeredness. True freedom comes from serving others and respecting both our own and others' dignity. True freedom enables us to grow as human persons.

Be Virtuous

---

*No man can purchase his
virtue too dear, for it is the only
thing whose value must ever
increase with the price it has
cost us. Our integrity is never
worth so much as when we have
parted with our all to keep it.*

\- Ovid

When someone uses the word virtue, we immediately form a mental picture of a saint or an unattainable standard, but that need not be so. Virtue is not necessarily the sole domain of religion or any moral philosophy, nor should its association with religion create a barrier to adopting virtue as a "Be."

It's helpful to examine the common critiques up front. Critics of the idea of virtue as a realistic, achievable standard of behavior dismiss the idea that humans have the innate ability to live virtuous lives. It would be naive to ignore the terrible offenses people commit against others and society, but the opposite is also true. There are just as many stories of valor, love, self-sacrifice, and generosity in the world as well. People are capable of great evil, but we are also capable of great virtue.

We know, from observing the world, that both are true, that evil and good coexist within humanity, so it makes sense that an admirable goal is to cultivate the good and weed out the bad in ourselves. When we nurture the goodness in ourselves and others, we call that goodness "virtue."

Every culture, community, and religion has its own idea of what virtue means. For example, in the U.S. Air Force, we define virtue as adhering to the Core Values: *"Integrity first," "Service before self,"* and *"Excellence in all we do.*" As an institution, the Air Force considers an Airman virtuous if he lives by the Core Values,

We can trace our modern concept of virtue back to the classical Greek civilization of in the 4th Century BC and the famous philosopher, Aristotle. He defined the classical ideal and what has become known as the "Cardinal Virtues." The word cardinal refers to the "principle" or "main" virtues, much like north, south, east, and west are the cardinal directions on a compass.

Aristotle's idea was that the highest calling was living a virtuous life, which perfected a person in the eyes of the gods as well as in the eyes of his fellow man. These ideas became so central to Western culture, that years later, when Christianity became dominant in political and philosophical thought in the Roman Empire, other philosophers like Augustine and Aquinas "baptized" the ideal of Classical Virtue and then added their own Christian-specific virtues called the "Theological Virtues."

The Greek philosophers Aristotle and Plato both agreed that virtue begins with the understanding of what the medieval philosopher Aquinas later called "first principles." First principles are the "universal human goods" that all humans aspire to and recognize as admirable. Aristotle's list included Life, Beauty, Love,

Truth, Creativity, Religion, And Sociability. The virtuous person protects and seeks to increase these universal human goods, while the imprudent person squanders them. While we probably rarely use the words virtuous and vice in everyday speech, we have all seen people whose choices we questioned. Social media and the paparazzi thrive on highlighting behavior that makes us wonder, "What were they thinking?" When someone gets in trouble or makes choices that harm their reputation, or others, those choices are usually a direct result of someone not exercising a virtue. In fact, we don't need a specific belief system or code of ethics to understand what's right or wrong-- although they certainly help as guides--those Universal Human Goods are written into our hearts.

For example, we know that defacing a natural monument or someone else's property with graffiti is wrong because it disturbs our sense of Beauty. We know betrayal of a loved one is wrong because it violates our sense of Loyalty. In addition, we know that lying to someone to cover up a crime is wrong, since it violates both Truth.

The Cardinal Virtues, sometimes also known as the Classical Virtues are the means which humans defend Universal Human Goods, our own humanity, and the health of society. The

Cardinal Virtues are prudence, justice, temperance, and fortitude. In the pages that follow, we'll spend some time thinking about how we can make virtue a real part of our lives and not just a slogan on a wall or worse, an unachievable goal.

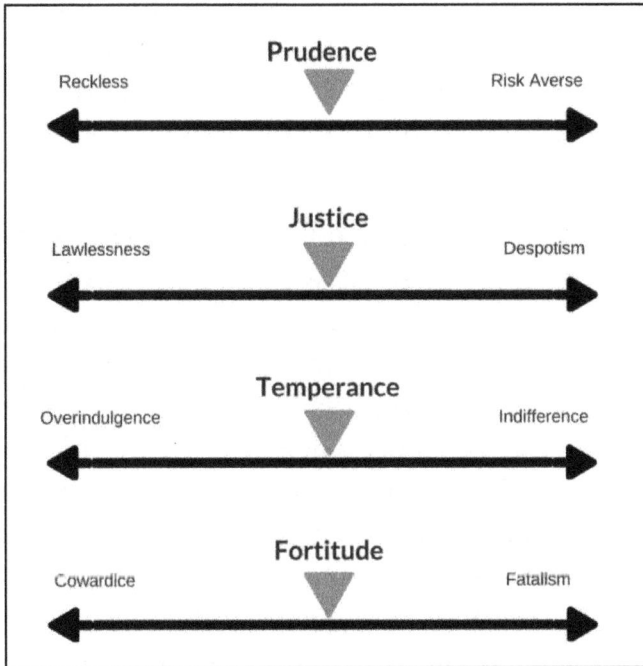

Figure 2. The Golden Mean

One last thought before we dive in, and that's the idea that virtue isn't in the extremes. Aristotle, and later Aquinas, also put forth the idea that *vice* lay in the extremes while *virtue* lived in the "Golden Mean." This means that, for example, *both* cowardice and fatalism are opposites of Fortitude. It's not that lawlessness isn't the opposite of Justice, of course it is, but so is tyranny.

Because only Good can create something, it follows that Evil can only twist things out of shape. If you're a fan of Tolkien's *Lord of the Rings* mythology, you'll recognize the principle immediately in the creation of the race of monsters known as Orcs. In the fictional Middle Earth, the evil Melkor created these pitiful and fearful creatures by torturing captured Elves, a beautiful and elegant race.

Virtue becomes vice in the same way. When the desire for Justice is warped into legalism, it no longer serves the Good but becomes of tool of the despot. If a soldier becomes a fatalist and no longer cares what happens to him, it's not Fortitude he displays when we exposes himself to danger. You get the idea. Authentic virtue seeks the good and avoids evil—and no amount of good intent can turn an evil act into a good one. Put another way, *intent* matters as much as the *objective nature* of the act. The virtuous person not only does good, he intends to do so by avoiding the extremes.

Prudence

Prudence is the ability for one to determine what's appropriate at any given time.

In the virtue of Prudence, we find the ability to make sound choices in the real world – choices that shield us from danger.

Having Prudence does not need to be a "weighty" way to live — it can be as simple as having good manners. When the choices are clear, then Prudence is an easy virtue.

For example, we all know serious acts, such as taking the life of an innocent person or stealing property are morally wrong. Only a sociopath would have difficulty discerning right from wrong in those extreme circumstances. Most daily choices aren't that clear cut. Friends sometimes put us in awkward positions by making questionable choices expecting us to approve or even go along. Other times people misbehave, and when they get away with it without penalty, it might cause us to question our own internal moral compass. Advice columnists make a very good living writing answers to the daily moral dilemmas that ordinary people face in their lives.

However, most of us don't have the luxury of clear-cut choices. We tell "white lies" to avoid hurting someone's feelings. Perhaps we sneak away after we bump someone's car and hope they don't notice the dent. These are everyday opportunities to increase our virtue if we truly value Truth, or become a little less human if we don't.

> *The character that takes command in moments of crucial choices has already been determined. It has been determined by a thousand other choices made earlier in seemingly unimportant moments… the decisions that, piece by piece, bit by bit, developed… habits of duty and honor and integrity—or dishonor and shame.*
>
> - Ronald Reagan

A personal story might be helpful here, as it illustrates a lack of prudence that could have cost me my life, and how the common choices we make sometimes have profound consequences.

My college friends and I were inner-tubing down the Guadalupe River near San Antonio, Texas and came upon the spot known as the "Blue Hole." It was a very deep spot in the river, and was probably connected to a subterranean aquifer. It was a local tradition for people to leap from an overhanging rock face into the Blue Hole. My initial answer to the challenge was, "No, thank you." However, once the boys swam away, leaving me alone with all the girls, my testosterone got the better of me and I raced to join them. I had a couple of chances to back out, including looking over the 20-foot drop-off, down to the water below. I didn't use the proper judgment – I wasn't prudent enough to back out, even though I really did not want to jump.

My companions counted to three and we all stepped off the precipice – it was then that I instantly regretted my decision. "This was a dumb idea," I thought as I plummeted to the water below along with six other boys, all within an arm's reach of each other. We hit the water so hard, and I went so deep that I nearly ran out of air before I made it back to the surface. There were a hundred things that could have gone wrong, and we were very lucky that no one was hurt. That experience was a great lesson in Prudence for me – that I should listen to my inner voice when it's shouting at me to pay attention

There are other ways to demonstrate Prudence besides deciding not to jump off 20-foot high cliffs. The virtue of Prudence is also helpful when making ordinary decisions, such as what to eat for dinner, or whether to accelerate through a yellow traffic light (or not). In fact, it's the daily small choices that define us far **more than the big ones.**

An imprudent person usually becomes that way through the accumulation of seemingly small choices over a period of time. The person with the lead foot has learned they can get away with driving as if they're on a race course because they've done it often enough for the habit to form. However, most people learn quickly, either through their own mistakes or someone else's, that refusal to obey traffic laws will result in speeding tickets, a wrecked car, or worse. These days, texting while driving is a far bigger problem than "merely" speeding. Prudent drivers put the phone away; imprudent ones attempt to operate a three-ton automobile with only one hand and one eye at high speed.

In short, I believe human beings innately understand the idea of "Universal Human Goods," which is why people follow similar moral standards, regardless of culture, upbringing, or religious tradition. It's also why Prudence is a virtue that's both achievable and universal.

Justice

Justice is the proper moderation between self-interest, the rights and needs of others, and rendering to each person what is deserved.

We most often think of "Justice in the legal sense: the system of enforcement of laws, including punishment for committing crimes. But the virtue of Justice is much more than merely administering laws and regulations. At a basic level, the essence of justice is that people are given their due. There is a measure of precision in Justice, because to do so requires a person to weigh and measure what another deserves. Unlike the other three virtues, which deal primarily with self-governing, Justice is a virtue that applies to how we treat others.

How does the ordinary person employ the virtue of Justice? Is Justice only for courts and police? Of course not.

Like all the virtues, the ordinary person can develop the virtue of Justice by treating others fairly in their common dealings. Paying a fair price for what you buy is Justice, as is repaying a loan promptly and in full. Taking responsibility for a failure in the workplace and not allowing another to take the blame is also a form of Justice. In fact, we can apply Justice in all our personal, professional and familial relationships. Justice need not have a negative connotation, such as "bringing a criminal to Justice." It can, and should be, a positive virtue where we understand and willingly accept our responsibilities to others.

Like all virtues, we can abuse Justice as well. If we weigh competing needs unequally, or a person's application or desire for justice overwhelms Universal Human Good (such as Truth), then Justice can easily transform into the vices vengeance or lawlessness. Justice as a virtue is not an end in and of itself – it is a means whereby we, as individuals and as a society, protect human dignity.

Justice's other traveling companion is Mercy. Mercy allows us to temper raw justice so we respect Universal Human Goods and inflict no unnecessary harm in the name of Justice. For example, in many countries, automobile operators are considered "professional drivers" and are *criminally liable* for vehicular accidents. Justice demands criminal sanction in some cases, but Mercy applied by those in authority, when appropriate, prevents people from going to jail for routine "fender benders." Raw Justice would fill jails; Mercy ensures only actual criminals go there.

Temperance

Temperance is the practice of self-control, moderation, and abstinence.

Whenever people think of the word Temperance, many probably think of Carrie Nation and Prohibition. While moderation or even abstention from alcohol can be Temperance, it's a narrow view of virtue. Temperance applies to keeping competing appetites in balance, like the way high-achieving athletes and scholars train their minds and bodies. In a few words, Temperance means governing your natural human appetites in a way that preserves freedom and prevents harm.

Researchers found that children with who practice good self-control, (i.e., typically better at paying attention, persist with difficult tasks, and suppress inappropriate or impulsive behaviors), are much more likely to find and retain employment as adults, spending 40% less time unemployed than those with a lower capacity for self-control.[7]

"All things in moderation" is a common phrase to describe Temperance, and it works in general. For example, an occasional glass of wine with dinner is fine and even thought to be healthy by some researchers. However, habitual excessive drinking is destructive to the body and relationships. Food is necessary for life, and good food is a pleasure–overindulging or eating unhealthy food intentionally is destructive. Even the Internet and video games can be transformed from a fun activity or useful tool into soul-crushing addictions if we allow it.

Temperance is the exercise of the will, to enjoy what's good without letting it become an addiction. There's nothing wrong with enjoying the good things in life; however, simple unhealthy attachment to things can become personally destructive.

For example, take the attachment to "stuff." Moving as often as I have during my military career, my family has had the unique opportunity to eliminate a lot of stuff. We have been fairly successful at paring our belongings down to a necessary minimum. This has been mostly voluntarily but sometimes involuntarily when things are lost or broken during shipment. Consequently, there are very few things that are truly precious to any of us, and the items that are precious to us have sentimental rather than monetary value. Each time movers (strangers) have come to my home to box up our household and then load everything onto a truck, we must come to grips with what's really important. We hold our breath and entrust those same strangers to deliver everything we possess to a new house, a new assignment. When the house is empty and the papers are signed, watching the truck drive away forces me to remember that "it's only stuff." Each time in this situation, my family is offered the opportunity to practice a little Temperance.

The opposite of people who are temperate with their stuff are hoarders. You might be familiar with the television show with that name. The people the cast and producers are trying to help, have let "stuff" completely take over their lives. By allowing their homes to overflow with possessions (and debris), they often forfeited relationships with family and friends, and frequently endangered their own health. Without Temperance and the ability to prioritize appropriately, competing appetites will control us until we are no longer free. Without Temperance, our own appetites and passions can enslave us and cause us harm.

Athletes understand this virtue very well, as they discipline their minds and bodies to achieve success in their sport. They may take on a special or restrictive diet, they may trade sleep for workouts, and they eschew certain celebrations, or even common comforts, to be their best. This sort of mental, physical, and spiritual preparation is a commonly proven way for athletes to succeed. We applaud that sort of self-control in them, but is it out of reach for us?

Of course not. We all have practice applying Temperance at a variety of levels. I believe the virtue of Temperance, applied in a sensible way that respects Universal Human Goods, is a necessary component to living a healthy adult life. Whenever we delay gratification or order our priorities toward a specific end, we are practicing Temperance. So, when we stay late to finish the presentation that is due tomorrow, we are subsuming our own personal comfort because others are counting on us. When we make sure to leave on time to meet our spouse for dinner, we are balancing our time for the spouse we vowed to "love, honor, and cherish." When we decline dessert so we can stick to our diet, when we turn off Call of Duty to help our kids with their homework, and when we delay our lunch to comfort a coworker having a bad day – those are demonstrations of Temperance.

Let Carrie Nation bury the hatchet; those with a proper understanding of Temperance will continue to grow and become "more free" by gaining an ability to control our own appetites.

Fortitude

Fortitude is defined as the forbearance, endurance, and ability to confront fear and uncertainty, or intimidation.

Of all the Cardinal Virtues, I think that fortitude is the easiest to understand.

When you have the virtue of Fortitude, you can see through the trials and tribulations of a task to the end goal, and the patience to endure the discomfort, or even danger that may accompany those trials. We value Fortitude highly in all occupations and walks of life and occupations, from those requiring physical labor to students "burning the midnight oil" to earn a diploma. Fortitude is merely the strength to endure hardship.

> *Every trial endured and weathered in the right spirit makes a soul nobler and stronger than it was before.*
>
> –James Buckham

In many professions and pursuits, leaders use hard work and even hardship as a tool to train individuals and teams to have self-confidence so they can achieve. The military uses shared hardship (physical exercise and restrictions on freedom) as a training tool in basic training with the specific purpose of creating a bond among the recruits. People often bond when they share and survive a tough experience. They also learn something in the experience as well: they learn they can "take" more than perhaps they originally thought they could. The same is true for an athlete; hard training improves an athlete's perception of what can be endured. They learn to adapt to the pain and stress of competition.

Military service and sports serve as useful examples, but what about the rest of humanity who are not preparing for combat or the Super Bowl? Fortitude is important for the "everyday person," since hardship is a part of ordinary life. Ordinary trials such as a new parent's sleep deprivation, cleaning up after a sick child, or pulling an all-nighter for a school project are all examples of when an ordinary person needs to exhibit fortitude.

We develop Fortitude, as with any other virtue, through the daily choices made on seemingly insignificant issues, which, over time, strengthen our constitution.

There's an adage in military training that's apropos: "In combat, no one rises to the occasion; they sink to the level of their training." This means that during stressful times or crises, we all revert to the way we have lived until that point. No one can discover the strength needed to endure a trial if they haven't suffered and endured trials in the past. This is the true reason self-denial is beneficial; it provides us with the training needed to make the best possible decisions during stressful situations rather than allowing situations or others to dictate what happens to us.

Wrapping Up Virtue

I hope you can see that authentic virtue is an achievable and even desirable goal. Virtue doesn't need to be feared. By safeguarding the Universal Human Goods through virtuous behavior, we improve ourselves and those around us. Virtuous people make their teams better, and those around them better, and they achieve more. Truly virtuous people can improve civilization, and live better lives.

Aristotle, and his successors like Plato, as well as the many others of philosophers and thinkers through the ages like Aquinas, all believed in virtues as an ideal person—and an achievable ideal. I firmly believe this is also true for us today. Of course, being human means being imperfect, so "all fall short," but isn't it better to *strive* for virtue and refuse to accept mediocrity? Virtuous people truly are happier in the long run. Short term vice may seem tempting, but ultimately, we end up only harming ourselves by failing to try for virtue. It's a 5,000-year-old straightforward prescription for living a healthy and successful life.

Be Balanced

Life is like riding a bicycle.
To keep your balance, you must
keep moving.

\- Albert Einstein

When my son was very young, he would give me the same advice as I left for work each day: "Goodbye, Daddy; have a good day at work. Be sure to drink your water, eat your lunch, and make new friends." Without realizing it, my son was encouraging me to live a balanced life. I always thought his farewell each day was far more insightful than just a small boy's simple advice. In fact, it's a great way to think about life balance.

There are many ways to understand and dissect the topic of life balance. My model consists of three focus areas: body, mind, and spirit. Others use health, wealth, and friends, or work/life. The U.S. Air Force has an outstanding approach to balancing the demands of work and life in their Comprehensive Airman Fitness Model, which takes the familiar mental, physical, and spiritual dimensions and adds a fourth, social. Additionally, there's the familiar Maslow's "hierarchy of needs" (Figure 1).

No matter how you slice up the facets of the human person, the takeaway is that humans are multi-dimensional. Therefore, we all should be deliberate about developing our whole person and not just one aspect. Each person has a body, mind, and the intangible part of themselves called a soul or human spirit. There is more to every person than meets the eye.

Figure 3. Maslow's hierarchy of needs (1943)

Being a well-rounded person means trying to determine what motivates and fulfills you, and then intentionally working to harmonize those very personal needs with the needs of your family, team, or workplace. It's more than a mere transaction; leaders must recognize that their team is more than names on an organizational chart. Each is a person with needs and aspirations of their own, who have come together to do a job for their own reasons. As individuals, we need to understand our personal engagement with those around us is just as important as our self-awareness.

The companies consistently rated "best to work for" seem to understand that idea. Those companies provide benefits that let the employees know they are valued for more than just their contribution to the bottom line, but also valued as people. In each case, the employees at the top-rated companies enjoy their work environment; the benefits provided are a bonus. The companies that treat their employees as whole persons, with more than a single dimension, are the ones who get the most engaged and involved employees, in return.

The next time you look at yourself in the mirror, stop for a minute and remember the words of my then four-year-old son: "drink your water, eat your lunch, and make new friends."

> *I believe that being successful means having a balance [in] life. You can't truly be considered successful in your business life if your home life is in shambles.*
>
> *– Zig Ziglar*

Living life balance is challenging. There are a lot of demands on a person's time: work, family, friends, hobbies, etc., and finding time to feed all aspects of the body and soul is key to any successful life. Anyone can put their head down and power through life, however, it takes a mature person to understand that how you live is equally important as what you accomplish. Keeping our lives in balance and living an integrated life is important to everyone.

To discuss life balance, we must have something to balance. Thinking about the human person in three categories provides a way to examine how to keep things in balance – and what will happen when we are unbalanced.

Humans are complex creatures that can be categorized in many ways. It's fair to say that each field of study, scientific or philosophical, has a unique way of looking at the human person. This is necessary since the attempt to synthesize all areas of study for humans is very complex work! I think that it is important to accept the underpinnings of the model before we begin tinkering with it.

The Human in Three Parts

"Be Balanced" refers to keeping all aspects of the human person in the proper perspective. There are many different models of human beings, from various personality and physical models to more esoteric ones. A common way to think about humans is to view each one as a composite of body, mind, and spirit. That is the model I will use to analyze life balance as a concept.

The first component of the human person is the Body, and it is where most people begin when getting to know someone. We will begin there. Bodies come in great variety: long, tall, short, round, male, female, and an almost endless assortment of skin colors. The biological definition of a person is the easiest, despite its multitude of categories, since the various characteristics that define a person's appearance, sound, and smell are available to us without any sort of intimacy.

We can feel another person using our senses without getting to know the person. Physicians, dietitians, physical therapists, workout trainers, and coaches all focus on the development and care of our bodies. Scientists classify the various branches of humanity through physical appearance: i.e., homo sapiens are distinctly different than homo erectus. Let us establish that one component of the human person is the body.

The second component of the human person is the Mind. Intuitively, we know we are more than just the sum of our physical parts. The philosophical maxim, *Cognito, ergo sum* (I think, therefore I am) is a testament to that intuition.

Since you are reading these words and processing them using the knowledge and experience that you have obtained through life experiences, you are validating that philosophical maxim. In addition to the biological and medical fields of study, we also have several areas of study dedicated to understanding the workings of the human mind. While psychologists are interested in the physiology of the brain, they are also interested in the study of the Mind.

The Mind is more than merely the electrochemical exchanges that take place in the brain. If that's all there was, it would be instinct rather than reason – "brain" rather than "mind." However, humans can reason, to retain information, to process and combine that information in new ways that enables further development. Our brains don't get physically larger, but our minds are constantly increasing in capacity as new information is absorbed and processed. Due to this demonstrated ability to process thoughts, data, and to learn, we can establish the second part of our human model, the Mind.

The third component of the human person is the Spirit. Are humans just thinking machines able to do calculus and able to lift rocks? I submit we are far more than thinking machines. We have a Human Spirit. To clarify, this is not about religion or even spirituality, although religion and spirituality are the Human Spirit seeking something greater than itself. This is the Human Spirit referenced as the human condition. Whether you are a person with religious beliefs, you believe in the Human Spirit--and I can prove it. Read on.

While we cannot physically observe the Human Spirit, we can view its effects and feel its presence in what medieval philosopher and theologian Thomas Aquinas named the 'Universal Human Goods'. Aquinas' idea is ancient, and springs from both Greek philosophy and the work of 5th century theologian and philosopher St. Augustine of Hippo.

"Universal Human Goods" are spiritual goods every human can relate to, regardless of whether you are a person of faith or no faith at all. "Universal Human Goods" are concepts such as Truth, Beauty, and Love. As humans with an immortal soul, we experience love for people and ideals, we delight in the beauty found in nature and art, and we demand and respect truth. While there isn't a definitive list of Universal Human Goods" the basics of truth, beauty, and love are sufficient to emphasize the argument that humans are more than mere flesh and blood.

Even the simplest of creatures can feel emotions, but only humans can feel Love with a "Capital L" in all its forms – from "brotherly love" to "erotic love" to "self-sacrificing love." Beauty is similar. Animals, plants, or even geology, can form beautiful things, simply as a byproduct of their existence. Only humans can create beauty. Furthermore, not only do humans create beauty for its own sake, but we also appreciate the beauty in nature. Humans seek out beauty in nature, art, each other, and celebrate that beauty, each in our own way.

As humans, we seem to have an innate appreciation for Truth as a "good" to be preserved. Even though humans can and do lie to each other, I have yet to meet a person of any sort who thinks that lying is a "good." A lie is sometimes necessary, but most people will go to great lengths to avoid lying for any reason.

While it is true that we can fabricate all sorts of reasons for humans to be truthful or to create beautiful things, it is also true that those things are not generated strictly from our intellect.

Truth, beauty, and love all come from the wellspring of the human soul, that immortal and spiritual essence that makes us human. Various efforts to scientifically analyze the human spirit has only gone so far – scientists have been able

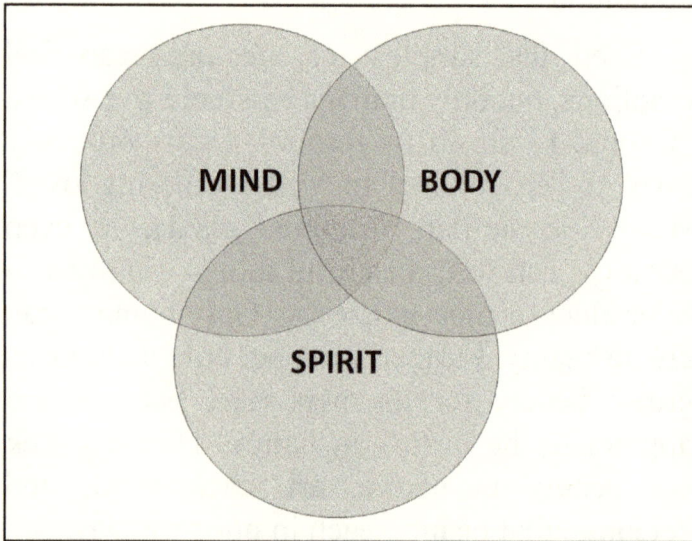

Figure 4. A model of the human person as relationship of mind, body, and spirit

to measure the weight of the human soul by weighing people before and after they die! All that being said, it should be obvious that if you have ever experienced love or beauty, clearly that appreciation came from a less tangible source than simply the brain or hormones—it came from your human spirit. Therefore, assembling all these "knowns" into a model, gives us Figure 2 below.

Much is written about the need for "life balance" and "work-life balance," but why should anyone "be balanced"? I propose that people are healthier and happier when we maintain a good balance of body, mind, and spirit; and we grow when we cultivate all three.

Consider the amount of time Americans spend at work. According to Hamermesh and Stancanelli (2014), paper entitled *Long Workweeks and Strange Hours*[8], it was found Americans tend to work longer hours and more "off" hours (such as weekends and evening). Does this sound like "balance" to you? Certainly, there are times when we need to work long hours to complete a project or do satisfy a customer's requests, but when almost a third Americans are routinely working weekends – more than any other developed Western country – then something is out of balance. Sometimes, it is easier to see when something is missing. So, what happens when we're not in balance?

The Body: The "Fitness Freak" and the "Couch Potato"

We only get one body, so we should take care of it. Can you go too far? Sure, you can. If you're devoting all your energy to enhancing your physique, with none left over for anything else, you're likely out of balance. I'm not taking about professional and Olympic athletes who spend a great deal of time staying in top physical shape. Clearly, those people are making short-term sacrifices for long-term goals and rewards. But even professional football players and Olympians make time for friends and family. They also make time to "recharge" by doing something else. Furthermore, professional athletes are also students of nutrition, physiology, and psychology, and incorporate that knowledge with their physical training.

This is not the case with the "Fitness Freak." The out-of-balance Fitness Freaks are not able to find the energy or time for anything else in their lives. Their entire self-worth is wrapped up in their appearance, performance, or both. These people are most likely the ones posting selfies constantly ("look at me!") or skipping out on a great experience because they cannot prioritize properly.

Fitness Freaks steer clear of relationships, because it consumes time "better spent" at the gym. These are people who are often thought of as shallow or one-dimensional. Aside from the spectacular exceptions, the Fitness Freaks' goal of perpetual youth is short-lived and eventually must fade, as the body's natural aging progresses.

In the extreme, the Fitness Freak can fall victim to all manner of self-destructive fad diets or even abuse drugs and supplements that promise fast results, but instead deliver destruction to the body the Freak is attempting to perpetually maintain. It should not take much convincing to see that as a poor way to live.

If the Fitness Freak's single-minded focus on the body is damaging, what about the other end of the spectrum – the "Couch Potato"? This is the person who doesn't exercise, eat properly, or get enough sleep. The Couch Potato will eventually lose their ability to engage in life. The lack of physical energy leads to emotional and spiritual energy drain, becoming a descending spiral of self-destruction, if a significant behavioral change is not made.

According to the World Health Organization (WHO), the Couch Potato's sedentary lifestyle significantly contributes to obesity, heart disease, loss of bone density, and eating disorders.[9] It is of such significance, that the WHO issued a health warning against the

Couch Potato lifestyle, listing it as one of the ten most significant health risks in today's culture.

The Couch Potato doesn't even have the (short-lived) benefits of the Fitness Freak's fit appearance. As the Couch Potato's health slowly deteriorates, they will withdraw further from life as they become less attractive to members of the opposite sex. As the slide into physical mediocrity increases, it becomes even more difficult for the Couch Potato to pull out of the dive and make a life change. At some point, only superhuman effort can enable the Couch Potato to reengage in life and start to live a balanced life.

What does a "body in balance" look like? As described with the various virtues, there can be a healthy compromise between the extremes of the Couch Potato and the Fitness Freak. We should strive to be healthy, make a conscious effort to eat right (most of the time), exercise appropriately for our level of ability, and improve ourselves physically. It doesn't mean we must all be athletes, but it does mean that we need to take care of the only body we will ever have.

The body-balanced person doesn't let their pursuit of health become a barrier to relationship. They engage with others, creating and maintaining bonds with family and friends, while keeping their passions in the proper context. The healthy person understands the connection between their body and the other elements of their person, preserving balance. A person with their body in balance is not afraid to have a piece of birthday cake, and is always encouraging others to engage in life. These are the people who not only stop to smell the roses, but also know where to find the roses in the garden.

The Mind: The "Poindexter" and the "Anti-Intellectual"

A "Poindexter" is someone who lives in their heads without any desire for human contact except online. Like the person with a bloated or anemic human spirit who lives in a parallel universe with no "worldly" concerns, the person who spends all their time improving their mind to the exclusion of all else, lives strictly in their own head. While expanding the mind by following intellectual pursuits is certainly good for an individual as well as society, there must be more to life than books and lectures. Balanced people do not live their entire lives in the world of the mind.

The stereotype of a person who lives in their head is often said to lack "common sense." The Poindexter knows only the theory and none of the practical application. While the Poindexter might know the principles behind the operation of an internal combustion engine, he or she probably would not know how to fix one. The Poindexter is often not comfortable with common human interaction, instead favoring books and spreadsheets, while posting online about fictional characters, rather than getting to know the cute girl sitting at the next desk. The Poindexter misses out on real life because they're too busy living in a fantasy world that they're reading about.

The "Anti-Intellectual" is the opposite of the Poindexter. They won't think in depth at all. The Anti-Intellectual sees no value in learning anything from books (or perhaps anything at all). The Anti-Intellectual actively scorns education as frivolous and a waste, claiming that intellectuals have no value. There is absolutely no room for discussion with an Anti-Intellectual. Once an idea is stored away in that

> *Don't confuse me with the facts; my mind is made up!*
>
> *- The Anti-Intellectual*

steel trap of a closed mind, no amount of facts will change their opinion. They listen to the same music, watch the same/similar television programs and only read material with the same viewpoint. If you have ever attempted to have a discussion on anything serious on Facebook, then you have probably met the Anti-Intellectual. Even sports analysis can get testy on social media!

What does a person with a balanced mind look like? They're alive, and they're attractive to others because of the way their life shines with energy and joy. A person with a healthy mind is willing to learn new things throughout their entire life. Many educational institutions aspire to develop life-long love of learning in their students. When reporters ask those who have lived exceptionally long lives what their secret is to reaching 90 or 100 years, many will say keeping their mind active is one of the most important factors.

> *"I'll never retire as long as I live – that's like retiring from life! I'll never stop writing, teaching, lecturing. If you're in good health, living is exciting on its own."*
>
> *- Bel Kaufman, 101 years*

A person who keeps their mind in balance, makes learning a priority, rather than an obsession. We should feed our minds good things, in the same way we feed our human spirits and bodies. Learn a language, read something new, go see a movie, talk to someone you don't know – these are just a few ways to help your mind grow. I find writing and travel to be two of my most effective tools for exercising my mind. Find a way that speaks to you.

Every summer, my mother would take my brother and me down to the local community center to pick out a summer activity. Sometimes, it was art lessons; other times, it was a physical skill such as archery or basketball. In each case, our mother wanted to be sure we engaged our minds over the summer break, and she was right to do so. She instilled in us a desire for life-long learning and curiosity about what was going on around us.

That's the strength of having a balanced and engaged mind: you develop a zest for life and both curiosity and a stronger connection to the world around you. The trick to having a healthy mind is to use it, realizing that you must engage in life, instead of just thinking about it!

The Spirit: The "Cloud Dweller" and the "Starving Soul"

Just like with the mind and the body, the spirit is balanced between extremes. The "Cloud Dweller" is someone who has overfed their spirit, living elsewhere while their body walks around on earth. The "Starving Soul" refuses to attend to their spirit.

When I talk about someone who is overfeeding their human spirit, I'm not talking about someone who is deeply religious. No one would ever accuse monastic religious communities of failing to live a balanced life. For example, the motto of the Dominican Order is *Ora et Labora*: a Latin phrase meaning, 'Pray and Work,' since all religious communities must support themselves even if they're cloistered in a secluded home. To be self-supporting, they farm, produce items that can be sold (such as beer and soap), and often work in their local towns and cities. The Daughters of St. Paul run bookstores and a publishing house; the Poor Clares of Perpetual Adoration run a TV station. In the East, Buddhist monks and nuns continue to work in the monastery and community as laborers and teachers.

A person who is overfeeding their human spirit is someone who lives in a way where the *well-being* of their body and mind are completely surrendered to an idealized spirituality. They come in two varieties: those that spend their days in their parents' basement engaged in lofty spiritual discussions but never actually doing anything, and the person who spends thousands of dollars in endless "spiritual pursuits" but never doing the actual work of spiritual growth.

In either variety, the Cloud Dweller refuses to tend to themselves or their surroundings. They fail to maintain relationships, and don't earn their keep. Like an overfed body, the overfed spirit becomes bloated and lazy – a lazy human spirit begins to turn on itself. Like the bloated couch potato body, the bloated human spirit doesn't do anything. The Cloud Dweller gazes endlessly at sunsets without preparing for the next sunrise. They don't have the energy to develop their human spirit, while still claiming to be "spiritual." The Cloud Dweller is sitting in place eating the spiritual equivalent of Twinkies and playing the spiritual equivalent of video games, getting spiritually fat. In short: they are stuck in their mother's spiritual basement going nowhere.

What about the person who lives with a malnourished spirit? I call those unfortunates Starving Souls with the same appearance as the person with the overfed spirit. Like the Cloud Dweller, the Starving Soul doesn't engage in life, but for different reasons. They're starving for the Universal Human Goods such as love and beauty, but lack either the capacity or will to obtain it. Without any nourishment for their Spirit, they're unable to generate the emotional energy needed to connect with others or the world around them.

To be clear, I'm not referring to a medical or psychological issue that inhibits people from being able to form bonds with others. Instead, it's the Starving Soul that keeps the Human Spirit unfulfilled. These poor souls are so malnourished that they're unable to accepted or appreciate the offered Universal Human Goods of love or beauty.

So, what does the healthy balanced person who feeds their human spirit look like? Their relationships and spiritual practices are energized, rather than weighted down. Just as a well-nourished person can enjoy rich fare on occasion, so can a well-nourished human spirit be open and accepting to greater, more powerful spiritual experiences.

Those who are spiritually well fed and balanced are generally happier and will seek out the opportunity to connect with others while engaging in life. The Universal Human Goods of beauty and love are appreciated and are sought within themselves and their surroundings. Their spiritual practices are part of the impetus of their lives, and help them grow. Just like supplying the body good food and exercise to make a healthy body, feeding the human spirit with beauty, truth, and love will make the human spirit healthy. Be inspired by something beautiful, cultivate friendships that give you energy, become part of something larger through service or volunteering. These are the things that expand the human spirit and keep you growing on the inside as well as outside.

Be Courageous

There are no easy answers,
but there are simple answers.
We must have the courage to do
what we know is morally right.

\- Ronald Reagan

There are as many definitions of the word courage as there are people. Courage can take many forms, but we generally think of courage in two main categories: physical courage and moral courage.

When we think about courage, the first image that comes to mind is the soldier or the first responder. We envision them facing danger to save the life of an innocent or defend their country from an unrelenting enemy. Perhaps we think about the terrible attacks of September 11, 2001 and the brave first responders racing up the stairs of the World Trade Center to rescue people trapped in the flames. Other cases include the spectacular heroism of the passengers of United Flight 93, regaining control of their aircraft from the terrorists but unable to prevent its tragic destruction.

Let's Roll!

There are also other forms of physical courage in the field of sports and adventure. Picture the big wave surfer riding the 40-foot face of a monster wave at Jaws off the Maui coast, or the climber conquering his own fear to scale the sheer cliff face. When we think of courage, we might picture something more comical, such as the Cowardly Lion from *The*

Wizard of Oz, where we can laugh at the vaudeville humor while rooting for the Lion to *find* his courage.

Physical Courage

Admiral Tarrant from the film *The Bridges at Toko-Ri* asked, "Where do we get such men?" The line is delivered near the end of the film, when the main character fails to return to the aircraft carrier after a mission, and Tarrant looks out at the busy deck and wonders where these men come from and why they serve. That question is a fundamental question people often ask of those who demonstrated courage, and then ask themselves when they look in the mirror. Maybe a better way to ask that question when applied to ourselves is, *"Where does courage come from?"*

I have given several examples of courage, but it's best to start with my preferred definition of courage

> *Physical courage is the ability to overcome fear and do what's necessary to survive, save a life, accomplish a mission, or excel despite physical or psychological barriers.*

Using this definition of physical courage obviously concerns overcoming *external* obstacles. To simplify, demonstrating physical courage is overcoming the "flight" instinct and choosing to *fight*. Physical courage results in facing danger or the threat of pain to accomplish a goal. Note the danger doesn't have to be *real*

– the mere *threat* of danger or pain can be enough to trigger a "fight or flight" response. What's more, "fight" doesn't necessarily mean a physical altercation or use of weapons. In the context of physical courage, "fight" simply involves meeting a challenge head on, without avoidance.

> *"Courage is doing what you're afraid to do. There can be no courage without fear."*
>
> *- Captain Eddie Rickenbacker World War I flying ace*

Let's return to Admiral Tarrant's question, *"Where do we get such men?"* or the rephrasing, *"Where does courage come from?"* There are several answers to that question; it's not as vague as you might think.

There's a physiological reason for courage. Researchers discovered by a unique (and bizarre) experiment involving snakes and an MRI machine. The Weizmann Institute of Science in Rehovot, Israel, strapped test subjects in an MRI machine with a snake suspended mere inches above their heads. Using the MRI to track brain activity, researchers identified the specific area of the brain associated with courage, the subgenual anterior cingulate cortex (SaCC). Using snakes to stimulate a fear response, test subjects reported their level of fear as the snake was moved closer and closer until their fear became greater than their courage.[10]

It's an interesting experiment. Just as researchers can determine the role that hormones and pheromones play in the attraction between boys and girls yet cannot define "love," neither can a purely physiological explanation satisfy our curiosity about the source of courage. As I have said many times before, humans are more complex than merely our biology. Surely biology can influence courage – a large person in a crowd of small ones is more apt to be courageous than the opposite. But when it comes to courage, biology is not the determining factor.

History is populated with stories of unexpected heroism from unlikely people. The 98-pound weakling who stands up to the bully on the schoolyard, and the grandmother who faces down the burglar are legendary, in part, because it has been documented and has repeated occurrences. It's a recurring theme in films about the plucky young person who saves the day while facing down a larger and more ferocious enemy. Do these real and fictional people have an oversized "courage center" in their brains? Perhaps, but I'd like to think it's more than that.

Can you learn to be courageous? More to the point, can you learn to control fear? Yes, you can. Learning to be courageous has a great deal to do with being prepared. When you have analyzed the "fight or flight" instinct as it relates to the situations you might face, you are much less likely to make a snap decision based on emotion, instead tapping into the wellspring of courage that all people possess. In a way, physical courage is the easiest to understand. We can see the danger being faced, and are able to prepare for it. We can physically prepare, mentally rehearse our response, hone our skills, and work in a team with others. This is applicable to battle scenarios, emergency situations, or even on the sports field. That preparation is key to suppressing the fear response.

When Air Force Academy graduate, former fighter pilot, and US Airways Captain Chesley "Sully" Sullenberger landed USAir Flight 1549 in the Hudson, he said in an interview with 60 Minutes that moments before the crash were "the worst sickening, pit-of-your-stomach, falling-through-the-floor feeling" that he had ever experienced. However, he and his crew had practiced emergency landings with such diligence, that they were able to put that fear aside and skillfully control the emergency landing. His team saved the lives of everyone on board the flight because they didn't succumb to fear. Instead, they controlled their fear.

The way the military values training, especially the repetition of so-called "perishable skills," is an indicator of the value of preparation. Soldiers expect to face danger, and prepare themselves against fleeing from it. The procedures are rehearsed over and over again until it becomes second nature.

I think courage comes from a well within our human spirit. It stems from more than mere biology, since we are more than mere flesh and bone. If humans were only biological machines, would there be an ability to create beauty, love, or be able to discern truth from lies? Biology certainly plays a role in who we are – after all, we are not disembodied spirits – but it cannot offer the entire answer. Courage, like other Universal Human Goods, comes from both our biology and our spirit.

A sense of duty and fraternal love contributes to courage, as does the nearly universal human social need to be accepted among a social group. Soldiers who exhibit courage in combat situations most often report that they were "just doing their jobs" and "didn't want to let their teammates down." We call that duty and loyalty; these qualities are among the most prized of human virtues.

People are willing to endure considerable hardship when they know that others are depending upon them. When that social pressure includes life and death situations, the sense of duty becomes even stronger. Oftentimes, our sense of duty –will override the fear instinct. That's where true courage originates. Ultimately, courage is an act of love. It's the love of others above self that will motivate people to endure hardship and brave danger to protect others. Without love, there can be no courage.

The Olympic gymnast is another example, though slightly different. The fear of injury and even death is real, but not from other teams. The gymnast must first conquer himself. In a real way, gymnasts must first conquer gravity before they can even approach the "inner voice." Like any sport, being an Olympic level gymnast requires constant dedication and sacrifice. It requires subordination of fear, heights, and pushing pain completely out of the mind to focus on the task at hand. In addition, teammates are depending on a high score. Years of 4 a.m. practices, foregoing social interactions and activities, arriving at the single moment where the difference between a gold medal and no medal is a fraction of a point. If the gymnast makes a mistake in the Olympics, he's not only risking injury, he's letting his country down.

Lastly, consider the courage of the cancer or rehabilitation patient. Both must rise daily with the knowledge they will face pain that day. For the cancer patient, that struggle is an actual fight for their life. Chemotherapy and radiation therapy are very hard to endure. There are days of nausea and pain each time. Choosing to fight their disease rather than succumb to it takes a daily dose of special courage. Similarly, the amputee or accident victim who goes to physical therapy knowing they face hours of pain just to hope they reacquire skills they once took for granted takes courage. Wounded Warriors in rehab face weeks or even months of painful therapy to learn to walk again, or feed themselves, or hug their loved ones. People who have suffered physical or psychological trauma must daily choose not to let their injuries define them. The alternative is to cease to live. That's courageous as well.

Overcoming pressure, the fear of mistakes, and the very real fear of severe injury requires physical courage. To be an Olympian is to find the courage to succeed even when success is elusive, to manage fear for years in a single-minded purpose to stand on the winner's podium.

Moral Courage

Moral courage is the companion to physical courage. There are hundreds of fictional examples in cinema and literature, as well as in real life. People who are willing to do the right thing or speak out against social injustice, while understanding that there might be a social or personal cost.

> "*Moral courage is the most valuable and usually the most absent characteristic in men.*"
>
> *- George S Patton Jr.*

There a plenty of examples all around us, people who have steadfastly held to their convictions, those who have chosen to speak up for those unable to speak for themselves. Saint Teresa of Calcutta actively confronted injustice and challenged the apathetic to act to help relieve the suffering of the people she served. Dr. Martin Luther King Jr. peacefully, but determinedly, required society to eliminate segregation, and treat all Americans as equals by the sheer force of his words and personal presence. President Andrew Johnson, who succeeded the slain President Abraham Lincoln, was determined to continue Lincoln's plan to "bind up the Nation's wounds" rather than subject the defeated South to prolonged military occupation and indignity. He suffered public ridicule and eventual impeachment by those in Congress who were motivated by revenge rather than the spirit of conciliation. These, and many others, are examples of heroic moral courage.

John Quinones of the television program *"What Would You Do?"* presents example after example of people "stepping up" to act when their morals or convictions are affronted. It is a comfort to me that, *most of the time*, people who find themselves in these types of situations choose to act, rather than let others suffer needless harm. When speaking of people who lack the moral courage to stand up to injustice, Quinones said, *"I think those of us who don't, and don't consider the consequences, have a lot to learn about how to love one another. Let's get involved in the world; let's make this a better place; let's give a damn."*

What is moral courage exactly? I have come up with a definition of my own, which is "The ability to hold firm to one's convictions in the face of criticism or personal attacks."

While only a few of us will ever have to charge into battle, rescue someone from a burning building, or compete in the Olympics, everyone has a daily opportunity to demonstrate moral courage. As the soldier physically and mentally prepares to enter battle, he also must prepare to be morally courageous when presented with the challenge. That sort of daily exercise of the moral courage "muscle" requires both a moral code and an external orientation. The ability to act or make the correct decision in stressful situations, like the fortitude required to become a champion athlete, requires repetition and practice. You can't just "start" to have moral courage any more than you can just show up and expect to compete in the Olympics.

How do you train to be morally courageous? First, you should have a solid moral foundation set in good character – a foundation based on a set of principles that are valued and worth defending. In the same way that it is impossible to stand steady on shifting ground, it's impossible to defend nonexistent values. That is the essence of moral courage: being willing to endure criticism and perhaps worse, to defend your convictions. Shifting values is called "moral relativism," while allowing the whims and social current to guide you is a road that leads to both sentimentalism and bullying.

To be clear, I'm not talking about maturing in your outlook on what's important to you, or even changing your mind. As we grow, we learn new facts, gaining new experiences that change our outlook on life. We learn to apply our principles in new situations, and we certainly encounter much more complex problems as we mature. Each of us should be able to appreciate the need to deal with things never conceived of in our youth as we mature. This is a skill that is particularly necessary for leaders. However, we will be unable to consistently make good moral decisions in unfamiliar circumstances if we don't have a firm set of starting values. The difference between the moral relativist and the principled person is the ability to make those difficult decisions unemotionally, even clinically.

> *"We are moving toward a dictatorship of relativism which does not recognize anything as for certain and which has as its highest goal one's own ego and one's own desires."*
>
> *- Pope Benedict XVI*

The principled person has two advantages over the moral relativist: they can use logic as well as the virtues of justice and prudence to make decisions, and they're able to make those decisions under pressure in new, never-before-encountered situations. Therefore, the principled person must have, what I call, an "external orientation."

Humans have the remarkable ability of being able to convince themselves of almost anything. It doesn't take much of an Internet search to see the extensive range of opinions on mundane topics such as diet and exercise, not to mention important subjects like government policy, religion, or scientific theory. Some of those opinions are informed, others – not so much. The interesting thing about this variety of opinions is the capacity for people to rationalize almost any position. Without a defined set of principles, decisions will be ruled by emotion ("it feels right!") or power ("I'm the leader; I decide!"). Even unarguable facts will not intrude on the moral relativist's decision-making process – as they conflict with the emotion of the moment or the leader's direction. Unless a moral relativist is willing to learn, facts don't matter. They will assume that the facts being presented are your opinions rather than facts, and therefore can be dismissed out of hand.

To understand the benefits of being a principled person, consider the analogy of a hike. Navigating from "here to there" along the trail requires the following tools: a map, a compass, and hiking skills. In this example, the map represents life, with marked dangers and trails to navigate. The compass's North Pole represents our principles. The skill at hiking equates to the experience and practice gained

while making decisions based on those principles.

Anyone who has spent any time in the outdoors knows not every danger is on the map – unexpected events will occur and dangers appear seemingly out of nowhere. Furthermore, a trail that looks easy on a well-made map is often confusing on the ground. When I was stationed at the Air Force Academy, I was amazed at the number of people who got lost on the "easy" trails due to taking a wrong turn. Even experienced hikers could find themselves lost on well-traveled trails when they didn't take routine precautions, were over-confident, and made additional bad decisions.

Usually, people would become disastrously lost because they had simply made a wrong turn, and then became disoriented and panicked. This situation is comparable to making an emotion-based decision. Emotion clouds our judgment, and prevents us from seeing things clearly (much like failing to simply retrace our steps on the trail to find the starting point). If you have ever been lost and been sure the way back was just ahead, you can appreciate the danger in allowing emotion into your decision-making process. Invariably, decisions made from emotion, rather than principles, are poor decisions that get us even more lost, rather than found. When you find, yourself experiencing an emotional response to a moral problem, stop and evaluate the situation in light of your principles.

Sometimes, the leader is the one responsible for getting lost. I was on a night hike along with others on Wake Island several years ago. When our beach trail was blocked, we elected to cut

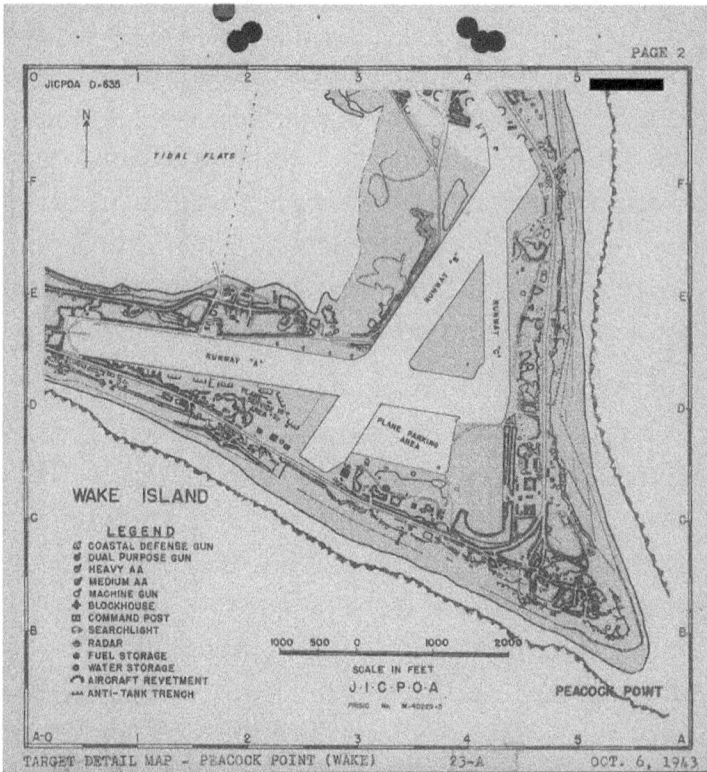

Figure 5. Map of Wake Island, Peacock Point Detail, 6 Oct 1943 (USMC Archives)

across the little island to find another trail – and ended up blundering through the dark jungle and over abandoned World War II trenches. There are any number of things that could have happened during that "boonie stomp" hike – almost all of them bad. Someone could have stepped on an unexploded shell, been bitten by a poisonous insect, received a gash from jagged rusty metal, or simply turned an ankle by falling into a hole or trench in the dark. Thank goodness we found the trail without any injuries or worse. But the reason we were "stomping" through the jungle in the first place was because we were following a leader who was certain he knew how to get back on the trail. None of us spoke up, even though all of us thought it was a horrible idea to get off the beach.

The moral dilemma analogy is a leader directing an action others in the group believe is morally wrong. If you're a principled person, you will have to take a stand if you're being led into a situation that could put you at risk of compromising your principles. To do that, you will need to have rehearsed how to properly use your map and compass.

Figure 6. Gen George S. Patton, Jr., USA

To become a principled person, you must practice what you believe daily. It does no good to hold onto a set of principles, if you keep them locked in a box and only take them out when you have a major dilemma. If the first time you look at your map and compass is after you are already lost, then there's no way that you will be able to determine where you are, let alone chart a course to your proposed destination. This means you need to have your map and compass ready from the beginning and refer to them often. You need to practice using your map and compass so that you know how they work and you'll be able to understand how to read the map.

Moral courage is like practicing those hiking skills. The daily exercising of the principles used to make moral decisions will make you more capable of making tough decisions as they arise. Is a boss asking you to violate your personal code of ethics or perhaps asking you to violate your morals? Are friends pressuring you to ignore your core values or go against your upbringing? Is a politician appealing to your emotions to gain your vote, despite his political platforms that are contrary to your principles? The only way you will know is if you check your "moral map and compass" to evaluate your position in relation to who you are as a person and where you want to be. To do that, you will have to have a working map and compass, have the skills to use them, and the strength and courage to hold onto them.

This is how moral courage is developed: by dealing with the small, seemingly insignificant decisions without stress or pressure. Do you perform the inspection, or just sign off on the form? Do you join in with the office gossip, or find a way to turn the conversation to something more productive or informative? Do you leave a note on the windshield of the car you accidentally bumped in the parking lot, or drive away? These are the types of everyday situations that can be used to exercise your "moral courage muscle." Making good decisions repeatedly will prepare you for the tough decisions in life, where the consequences are far more severe. I know it sounds obvious, but if you truly want to be a person of good character, a morally courageous person – then you must work on it daily. Choose your path, align your compass to the North Star of your principles, and stay on the trail.

Summing It Up

---

*Don't fear failure so much
that you refuse to try new things.
The saddest summary of a life
contains three descriptions:
could have, might have, and
should have.*

-Louis E. Boone

No person is perfect, but that lack of perfection should not give us permission to live in mediocrity. The Five Be's is a prescription against mediocrity, and provide us with a vision of who we can be, when we are at our best. **Be Proud of Who You Are,** especially when others try to devalue you. **Be Free** of the chains of others' desires or your own appetites: you are so much more! **Be Virtuous** and remember that virtues are like the guardrails on the road of life: there to keep you safe rather than hem you in. **Be Balanced** and live a life of significance by developing your whole person, not just a portion of yourself. Finally, **Be Courageous** because to live a balanced and integrated life of virtue in authentic freedom *requires* courage.

You have it in you – unleash the authentic person you know you can be!

Order Form

Email Address: _____

Daytime Phone: _____

Billing Address

Name: _____

Street Address: _____

City / State / Zip: _____

  Country: _____

Shipping Address (if different than Billing Address)

Name: _____

Street Address: _____

City / State / Zip: _____

  Country: _____

Payment Information:

Qty: ____ X $19.95   = _____

Plus Shipping @$2.50/book   = _____

                  TOTAL = _____

Credit Card: MC/Visa Number: _____

Exp: _____ Security Code: _____

Scan and email to: Mickey@LeadTheWayMedia.com

www.mickeyaddison.com

Other Books by Mickey

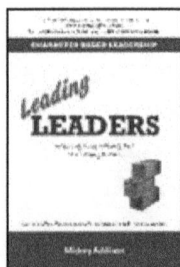

Leading Leaders: Inspiring, Empowering, and Motivating Teams

Leading Leaders is straightforward advice for leaders at every level on how to become successful. Developed over a 30-year military career and a lifetime of leading, Colonel Mickey Addison lays out the foundation for character-based leadership. Illustrated through personal stories and anecdotes, *Leading Leaders* is a must-read for anyone who wants to improve their productivity and their character. *vailable in both ebook and paperback.*

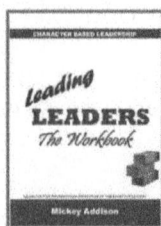

Leading Leaders: The Workbook

Leading Leaders: The Workbook is a companion to Mickey Addison's acclaimed work by the same title, but can be used as a stand-alone guide for discussion groups, seminars, and individual study. Thoughtful questions and chapter self-assessments will assist leaders and teams to improve their leadership skills through candid review of both leadership and followership skills.

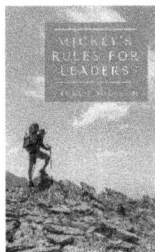

Mickey's Rules for Leaders

Developed over career spanning three decades, Colonel Mickey Addison gives leaders a "how to" rule book for leading at any level. The eleven rules in the book are excellent guidelines for relating to other people, correctly prioritizing work, and leading teams to high performance. Learn the secrets of leadership from a leader who's lived it! With Rules like "Don't Spook the He rd" and "The First Report is Usually Wrong", this is not your average handbook! *Available in both ebook and paperback.*

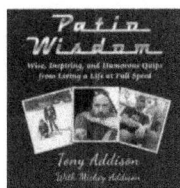

Patio Wisdom: Wise, Inspiring, and Humorous Quips from Living a Life at Full Speed

Welcome to the world of The Patio King! Inside are the musings from Living a Life at Full Speed, where wisdom comes from the School of Hard Knocks. Its wisdom born of adventure and hardship, joy and pain, victory and defeat…and everything in between. Illustrated with the author's own photos, and narrated with quips and memories, *Patio Wisdom* will leave you in tears and stitches.

All of Mickey's books are available at his website: www.mickeyaddison.com

About the Author

Mickey Addison believes anyone can reach high performance if inspired and led. As a 30-year veteran of the US Air Force, he's had decades of experience leading diverse teams of thousands. Mickey is an author, blogger, and a frequent contributor to military newspapers and journals. He's also frequent guest on radio and podcasts. His passion for leadership led him to found his own publishing company, and Mickey is also a regular contributing author at GeneralLeadership.com.

Mickey is passionate about inspiring people to be their best and leading organizations to high levels of performance. As an Air Force officer, Mickey has handled national portfolios totaling billions of dollars. He's presented on dozens of topics to senior leaders in the military, industry, state, and federal government, and worked with international business and government executives and in a dozen countries in Asia, Europe, and the Middle East.

For speaking, consulting, or writing, contact Mickey via email at Mickey@leadthewaymedia.com, or through his website: mickeyaddison.com.

Index

"fight or flight", 83, 85
"What Would You Do?", 90
A'ama Crabs, 20
Abraham Lincoln, 89
addiction, 25, 26, 27, 46, 111
Addiction, 26, 27, 111
Airman, 2, 5, 8, 9, 10, 13, 14, 19, 31, 35, 56
Alamihi Crab, 21
Anti-Intellectual, 70, 71
Aquinas, 35, 62
Aristotle, 31, 35
athletes, 45, 48, 66, 68
Athletes, 48
Authentic pride, 19, 20
Beauty, 36, 62
Body, 60, 66
boundaries, 2, 3, 4, 5
Buddhist monks, 74
cancer, 88
Cardinal Virtues, 35, 36, 50
Carrie Nation, 45, 49
Cloud Dweller, 74, 75
Cognito, ergo sum, 61
compass, 35, 39, 94, 97, 98, 99
core values, 98
Couch Potato, 66, 67, 68
courage, x, 80, 82, 83, 84, 85, 86, 87, 88, 89, 90, 91, 98, 102
daily choices, 39, 51
daily small choices, 42
Daughters of St. Paul, 74
dignity, 3, 17, 18, 19, 32, 44
drug abuse, 67
ethics, 36, 98
Fitness Freak, 66, 67, 68

Fortitude, 50, 51, 53
freedom, 5, 11, 24, 25, 27, 28, 30, 31, 32, 45, 47, 49, 51, 102
freedom to travel, 29
Freedom, 24
good character, 91, 99
gravity, 28, 87
healthy mind, 72, 73
healthy people, 16
healthy person, 69
hoarders, 47
human spirit, xi, 56, 64, 70, 74, 75, 76, 77, 86
John Quinones, 90
Justice, 43, 44
life balance, 56, 58, 59, 60, 65
Love, 62
Manners, 3
military, 8, 9, 10, 13, 19, 31, 32, 46, 50, 51, 86, 90, 104, 107
Military service, 51
military standards, 32
moral courage, 80, 91, 99
moral dilemma, 97
moral problem, 95
moral relativist, 92, 93
Mother Teresa of Calcutta, 89
Olympic, 66, 87
online, 70, 111
Ora et Labora, 74
overfed spirit, 75
paparazzi, 36
Poindexter, 70, 71
Pray and Work, 74
pride, 10, 11, 12, 13, 14, 15, 19, 20, 21

principled person, 92, 93, 97
proud, 5, 8, 9, 10, 11
Prudence, 37, 39, 40, 41, 42, 92
relationships, 12, 25, 43, 45, 47, 66, 75, 76, 111
religion, 14, 34, 36, 62, 93
sacrifices, 66
San Antonio, 40
self-esteem, 11, 16
self-worth, 11, 12, 16, 17, 20, 21, 66
Self-worth, 18
sense of duty, 86, 87
Spirit, 62, 74, 76
spiritual, 48, 56, 62, 64, 67, 75, 76
spiritual energy drain, 67
spiritually well fed, 76
sports, 17, 20, 51, 71, 80, 85
standards, 4, 5, 31, 42
stereotyping, 8
Sullenberger, 85
team, 9, 11, 13, 15, 20, 57, 85, 86
Temperance, 45, 46, 47, 48, 49

temperate, 47
The Bridges at Toko-Ri, 82
The Wizard of Oz, 81
top-rated companies, 58
United States Air Force, vi, 2, 8, 9, 10, 13, 14, 31, 34, 35, 56, 85, 95, 107
Universal Human Goods, 36, 42, 44, 48, 53, 62, 76, 86
    Beauty, 63
    Love, 63
    Truth, 36, 40, 44, 62, 63, 64
vice, 14, 31, 36
virtue, 13, 15, 31, 34, 35, 36, 39, 40, 41, 42, 43, 44, 45, 48, 50, 51, 53, 102
vision, xi, xiii, 4, 5, 102
voluntarily, 46
well-rounded person, 57
white lies, 39
World Health Organization, 67
World War II, 96
Wounded Warriors, 88
zest for life, 73

End Notes

1. A Japanese term for the man who works in an office, and is wholly dedicated to his company even at the cost of his health and relationships.

2. University of British Columbia. "Pride May Not Come Before A Fall, After All." ScienceDaily. 18 June 2007. www.sciencedaily.com/releases/2007/06/070615214643.htm

3. U.S. Department of Health and Human Services. *The Health Consequences of Smoking—50 Years of Progress. A Report of the Surgeon General.* Atlanta, GA: U.S. Department of Health and Human Services, Centers for Disease Control and Prevention, National Center for Chronic Disease Prevention and Health Promotion, Office on Smoking and Health; 2014. www.surgeongeneral.gov/library/reports/50-years-of-progress/full-report.pdf.

4. National Survey on Drug Use and Health (NSDUH), 2013, National Institute on Drug Abuse, online, accessed 20 Sep 15, http://www.drugabuse.gov/publications/drugfacts/nationwide-trends.

5. Alarming Video Game Addiction Statistics, Addictions.com, online, accessed 20 Sep 15, <http://www.addictions.com/video-games/alarming-video-game-addiction-statistics/>.

6. John Fabry, Allison Miller, Allison Milwid, Videogame Addiction Helpline, University of Pittsburgh, 2008, online, http://people.cs.pitt.edu/~mehmud/cs134-2084/projects/Epic_Fail/about.html.

7. Association for Psychological Science. "Childhood Self-Control Linked to Enhanced Job Prospects Throughout Life." ScienceDaily. 14 April 2015, www.sciencedaily.com/releases/2015/04/150414130403.htm.

8. Long Workweeks and Strange Hours, Daniel S. Hamermesh, Elena Stancanelli, NBER Working Paper No. 20449, Issued in September 2014, http://www.nber.org/papers/w20449.

9. "Physical Inactivity a Leading Cause of Disease and Disability, Warns WHO" World Health Organization Media Center, 4 April 2002, online, accessed 20 Sep 15, http://www.who.int/mediacentre/news/releases/release23/en/.

10. Rachael Rettner, "Brain's Courage Center Located," LiveScience.com, 23 June 2010, online, accessed 20 Sep 15, http://m.livescience.com/8342-brain-courage-center-located.html, accessed 20 Sep 15.

www.ingramcontent.com/pod-product-compliance
Lightning Source LLC
Chambersburg PA
CBHW030419100426
42812CB00028B/3018/J